The Little Book of
THE WHITE HOUSE

By Zack Bush and Laurie Friedman
Illustrated by Vitor Lopes

DEDICATED TO YOU –
OUR WONDERFUL READER

THIS BOOK BELONGS TO:

_____

The **WHITE HOUSE**, which is located in our nation's capital—Washington, DC—is the official residence of the president of the United States.

The president and the president's family live there, and the president works there too. The **WHITE HOUSE** is one of the most famous American landmarks.

There's so much to know about it. Ready to learn more? Just turn the page!

But it wasn't completed until 1800.
That's when President John Adams
became the first American president
to live in the **WHITE HOUSE**.

Since then, every American president has lived in the **WHITE HOUSE**!

Over the years, the **WHITE HOUSE** has changed and grown. Today, there are 6 floors, 132 rooms, 35 bathrooms, 28 fireplaces, and 8 staircases in the **WHITE HOUSE**.

If you wanted to play a game of hide-and-seek in the **WHITE HOUSE**, you would have lots of places to hide!

The **WHITE HOUSE** is also famous for its beautiful landscaping and gardens.

The Rose Garden is near the West Wing of the **WHITE HOUSE**, where the president works.

And the Kitchen Garden is where vegetables, fruits, and herbs are grown to feed the president's family and guests of the **WHITE HOUSE**.

Twice a year—once in the spring and once in the fall—the grounds of the **WHITE HOUSE** are open for the public to see the beautiful gardens.

The **WHITE HOUSE** has many special rooms where the president of the United States works, lives, and entertains guests.

The Oval Office, the official office of the president, is located in the West Wing.

The president is not the only person who works in the **WHITE HOUSE**.

There are also offices in the East and West Wings of the **WHITE HOUSE** for the president's staff, the First Lady, and the vice president.

It takes lots of people to run a country!

The second and third floors of the **WHITE HOUSE** are where the president and his family live.

Here's a fun fact: the **WHITE HOUSE** has its own movie theater, bowling alley, swimming pool, tennis court, running track, and library. There's even a doctor's office, a dentist's office, and a barber shop!

Many rooms in the **WHITE HOUSE** are used by the president for entertaining.

The East Room is the largest room, and it is where parties and dances take place.

The State Dining Room is where official dinners are held. As many as 140 people can sit down to eat a meal together.

The Green, Blue, and Red rooms are named for the colors that were used to decorate them.

Every year, over one million tourists visit the **WHITE HOUSE**.

Whether you visit the **WHITE HOUSE**, read about it from home, or study it at school, there are so many interesting facts you can learn.

Like many buildings, the **WHITE HOUSE** has been expanded and remodeled over time.

In fact, the original building was almost entirely rebuilt in 1814 after the British burned it down during the War of 1812.

Lots of kids and grandkids of American presidents have lived or spent time in the **WHITE HOUSE**.

And pets have lived there too, including dogs, cats, snakes, badgers, birds, and even guinea pigs!

The address of the **WHITE HOUSE** is 1600 Pennsylvania Avenue. It is so big and so important that it has its own postal code.

If you want to send a letter to the **WHITE HOUSE**, be sure to address it to:

Here's one last fun fact about the **WHITE HOUSE**.

If you were going to paint the outside of it, you would need over 500 gallons of paint. That's a lot of paint!

CONGRATULATIONS!

Now you know so much about the **WHITE HOUSE**.

Here's your **WHITE HOUSE** badge.
Go ahead. Print it out, pin it on, and maybe one day
you will get to visit this special landmark.

Go to the website www.BooksByZackAndLaurie.com
and print out your badges from the
Printables & Activities page.

And if you like this book, please go to
Amazon and leave a kind review.

Keep reading all of the books in #thelittlebookof series to learn new things and earn more badges. Other books in the series include:

VALUES/EMOTIONS	ACTIVITIES/IDEAS
The Little Book of Kindness	The Little Book of Camping
The Little Book of Patience	The Little Book of Sports
The Little Book of Confidence	The Little Book of Music
The Little Book of Positivity	The Little Book of Government
The Little Book of Love	The Little Book of Transportation
The Little Book of Good Deeds	The Little Book of Presidential Elections
The Little Book of Responsibility	The Little Book of Grandparents
The Little Book of Curiosity	The Little Book of Bedtime
The Little Book of Gratitude	The Little Book of Good Manners
The Little Book of Friendship	The Little Book of Dance
The Little Book of Laughter	The Little Book of Yoga
The Little Book of Creativity	The Little Book of Healthy Habits
The Little Book of Honesty	The Little Book of Setting Goals
The Little Book of Imagination	The Little Book of Organization
The Little Book of Happiness	The Little Book of Teamwork
The Little Book of Sharing	The Little Book of Baking
The Little Book of Listening	The Little Book of Cooking
The Little Book of Hope	The Little Book of Mindfulness
The Little Book of Cooperation	The Little Book of Adventure

SCIENCE/NATURE

The Little Book of Nature
The Little Book of Outer Space
The Little Book of Going Green
The Little Book of Weather
The Little Book of Pets
The Little Book of Dinosaurs
The Little Book of Plants

MILESTONES/HOLIDAYS

The Little Book of Kindergarten
The Little Book of First Grade
The Little Book of Valentine's Day
The Little Book of Father's Day
The Little Book of Halloween
The Little Book of Giving (Holiday Edition)
The Little Book of Santa Claus
The Little Book of Back to School

LANDMARKS/DESTINATIONS

The Little Book of the Supreme Court
The Little Book of the Grand Canyon
The Little Book of the Statue of Liberty
The Little Book of the White House

Made in the USA
Middletown, DE
11 September 2024

60826480R00022